THURGOOD

For Rhys

A special thanks to Bryan Stevenson,
the Thurgood Marshall of our era, for lending his
critical eye to this book in advance.
—J.W.

For everyone—may you be inspired to seek truth and
find courage, and like Thurgood Marshall, prove to the world
that justice is what love looks like in public.
—B.C.

 Published in the United States by Schwartz & Wade Books,
an imprint of Random House Children's Books, a division of Penguin Random House LLC, New York.
Schwartz & Wade Books and the colophon are trademarks of Penguin Random House LLC.
Visit us on the Web! rhcbooks.com
Educators and librarians, for a variety of teaching tools, visit us at RHTeachersLibrarians.com
Library of Congress Cataloging-in-Publication Data
Names: Winter, Jonah, author. | Collier, Bryan, illustrator.
Title: Thurgood / Jonah Winter, Bryan Collier.
Description: First edition. | New York: Schwartz & Wade Books,
an imprint of Random House Children's Books, a division of Penguin Random House, 2019.
Audience: Grades K-3. | Audience: Ages 5-9.
Identifiers: LCCN 2018053004 | ISBN 978-1-5247-6533-0 (hardcover)
ISBN 978-1-5247-6534-7 (hardcover library binding)
ISBN 978-1-5247-6535-4 (ebook)
Subjects: LCSH: Marshall, Thurgood, 1908-1993—Juvenile literature. | African American judges—Biography—Juvenile literature.
United States Supreme Court—Biography—Juvenile literature.
Classification: LCC KF8745.M34 W56 2019 | DDC 347.73/2634 [B]—dc23
The text of this book is set in Interstate.
The illustrations were rendered in watercolor and collage.
MANUFACTURED IN CHINA
10 9 8 7 6 5 4 3 2 1
First Edition
Random House Children's Books supports the First Amendment and celebrates the right to read.

THURGOOD

by **Jonah Winter** illustrated by **Bryan Collier**

schwartz & wade books new york

Normally, you don't look at a sandbox full of toddlers and say, "Little Jimmy there is going to become a world-famous lawyer!" But there was this little boy named *Thoroughgood* who was by all accounts a *born lawyer*. The first evidence? At age six, he convinced his parents to *legally* change his name—to *Thurgood*.

Well, this Thurgood character would grow up to change more than just his name—he would change the law of the land.

Here are the facts of his case: *It's 1922. Baltimore.*

A fifteen-year-old black kid is trying to get on a trolley with an armload of hatboxes he has to deliver.

He accidentally bumps into a white woman. A white man calls him a hateful word and shoves him off the trolley.

The kid, whose dad has taught him never to take that kind of abuse, punches the man and gets arrested—even though he's just fifteen and was acting in self-defense. His white boss comes to the jail and manages to get him released. The kid's name: Thurgood Marshall. For Thurgood, such things are just a fact of life.

FACT: As a black kid growing up in America during the 1920s, Thurgood was forced to attend a blacks-only school called Colored High School. Unlike Baltimore's all-white schools, it had no library, gym, OR cafeteria. It was so overcrowded that half the students had to go in the morning and half in the afternoon.

FACT: From a classroom window, Thurgood could hear the sounds of the white cops beating confessions out of black suspects in the police station across the street. This was the world he was born into: a world where black people had few legal rights.

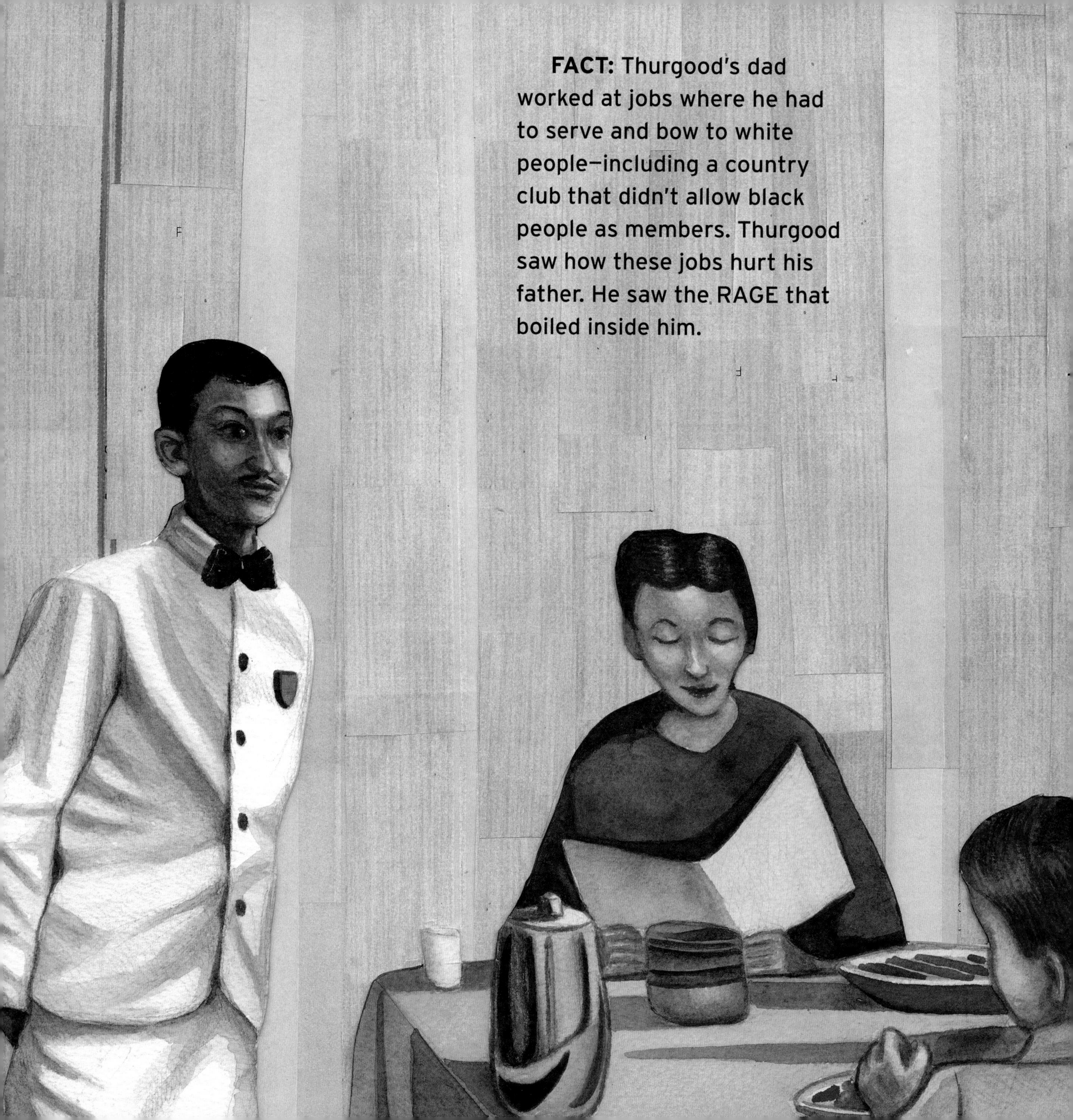

FACT: Thurgood's dad worked at jobs where he had to serve and bow to white people—including a country club that didn't allow black people as members. Thurgood saw how these jobs hurt his father. He saw the RAGE that boiled inside him.

But he also learned some things from his dad. He learned about courtrooms and lawyers. His father used to take him to trials, and there they would sit, watching lawyers argue about justice and injustice, guilt and innocence, truth and falsehood.

Back at home, over dinner, his dad would engage him in arguments about these trials, about the news, about anything. He would raise his voice, demand that Thurgood back up his points with evidence. And Thurgood would put it right back to him, word for word, point for point—with glee, with fire.

LINCOLN

As it turned out, this sloppy kid with untucked shirts and ink-stained pockets had a knack for arguing. He became captain of his high school debate team—unparalleled in his debating AND talking skills. He gave epic classroom presentations—so long that his teachers would have to cut him off! No one could outtalk Thurgood—especially once he went to college, at Lincoln University, in Pennsylvania, where right away he made his mark as the loudest talker, funniest joke-teller, and best arguer of them all. As the star of his college debate team, he earned the nickname "the Wrathful Marshall."

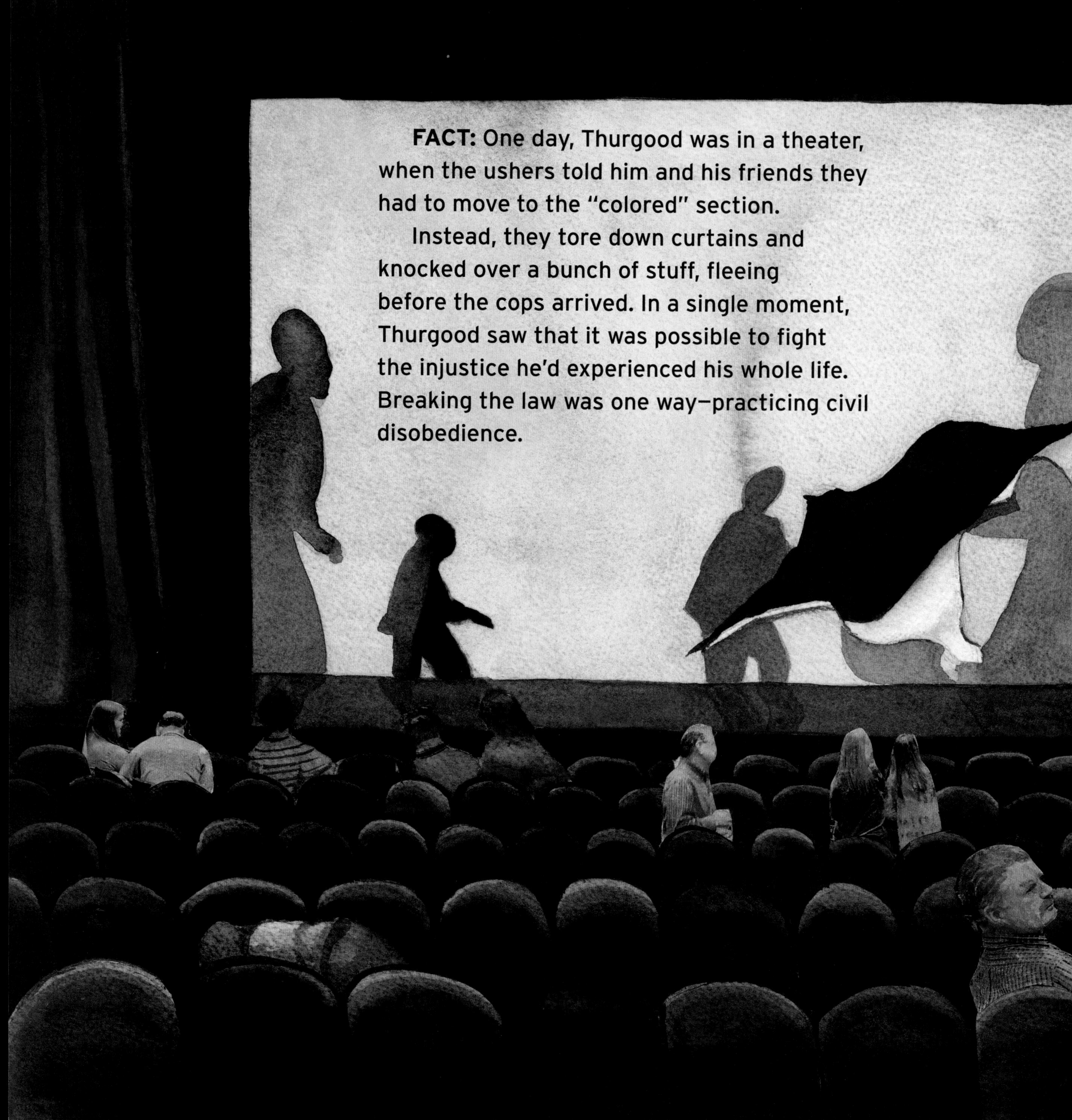

FACT: One day, Thurgood was in a theater, when the ushers told him and his friends they had to move to the "colored" section.

Instead, they tore down curtains and knocked over a bunch of stuff, fleeing before the cops arrived. In a single moment, Thurgood saw that it was possible to fight the injustice he'd experienced his whole life. Breaking the law was one way—practicing civil disobedience.

COLORED
NTRANCE

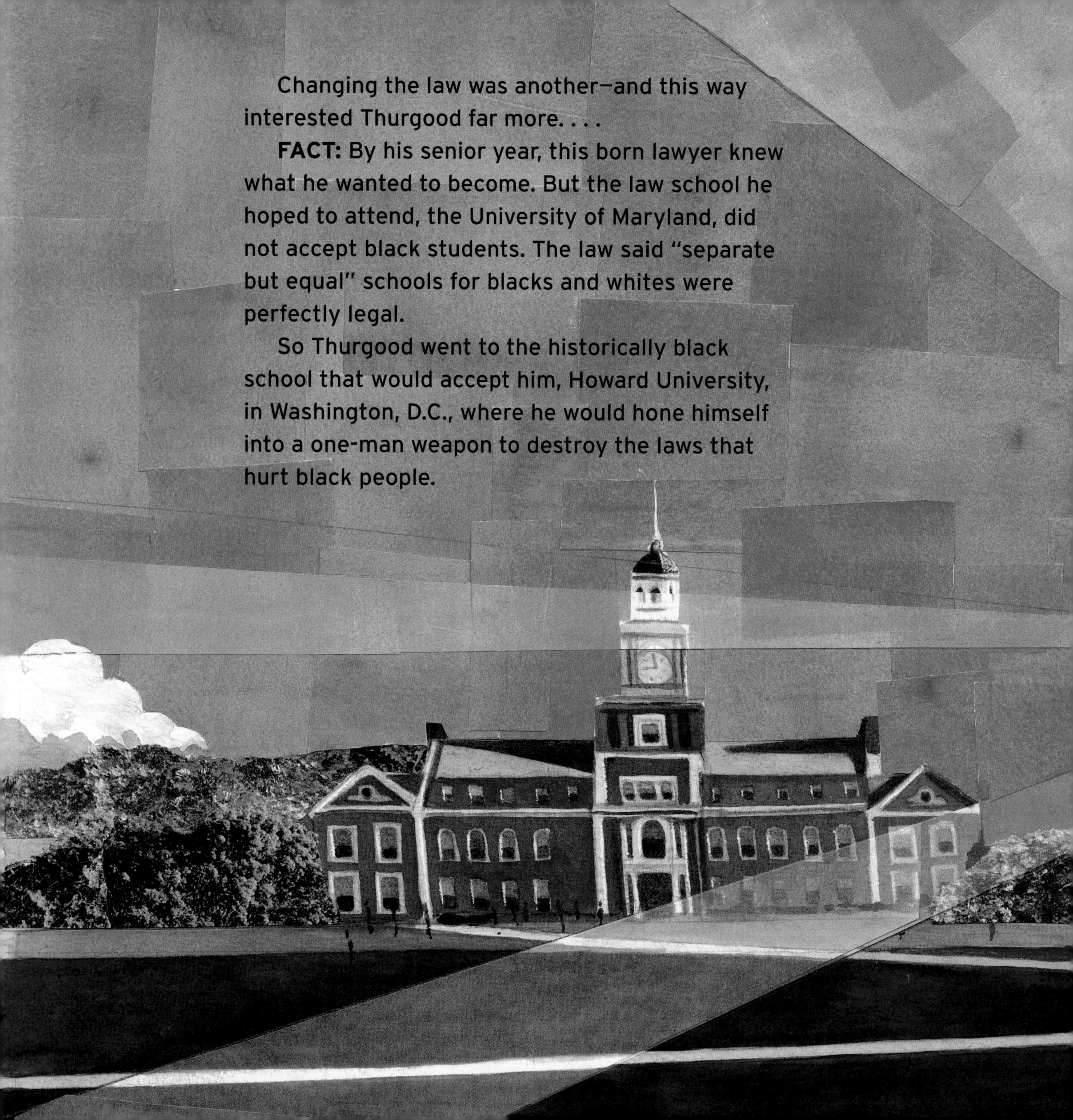

Changing the law was another—and this way interested Thurgood far more. . . .

FACT: By his senior year, this born lawyer knew what he wanted to become. But the law school he hoped to attend, the University of Maryland, did not accept black students. The law said "separate but equal" schools for blacks and whites were perfectly legal.

So Thurgood went to the historically black school that would accept him, Howard University, in Washington, D.C., where he would hone himself into a one-man weapon to destroy the laws that hurt black people.

4+4=

He became the star pupil of the great civil rights lawyer Charles Houston, who trained his students to challenge legalized racial segregation—enforced separation.

Houston took Thurgood on a road trip to the Deep South to study the segregated schools for black and white kids.

FACT: Unlike the white kids' schools, the black kids' schools had dirt floors and no restrooms. The students were malnourished and sad. "Separate but equal"? Yeah, right.

Well. Can you guess what Thurgood's first major legal battle was once he'd graduated and become a lawyer? It was against the very law school that would not accept him because of his skin color.

A lawyer's job is to convince a judge or a jury of what is just and unjust, true and untrue. It is to present facts and evidence. Thurgood presented the facts: The University of Maryland had no legal right to bar his black client from its law school. As a citizen of the United States, he was entitled to equal treatment because of the Equal Protection Clause in the Fourteenth Amendment to the U.S. Constitution.

VERDICT: The law school would have to accept black students—victory.

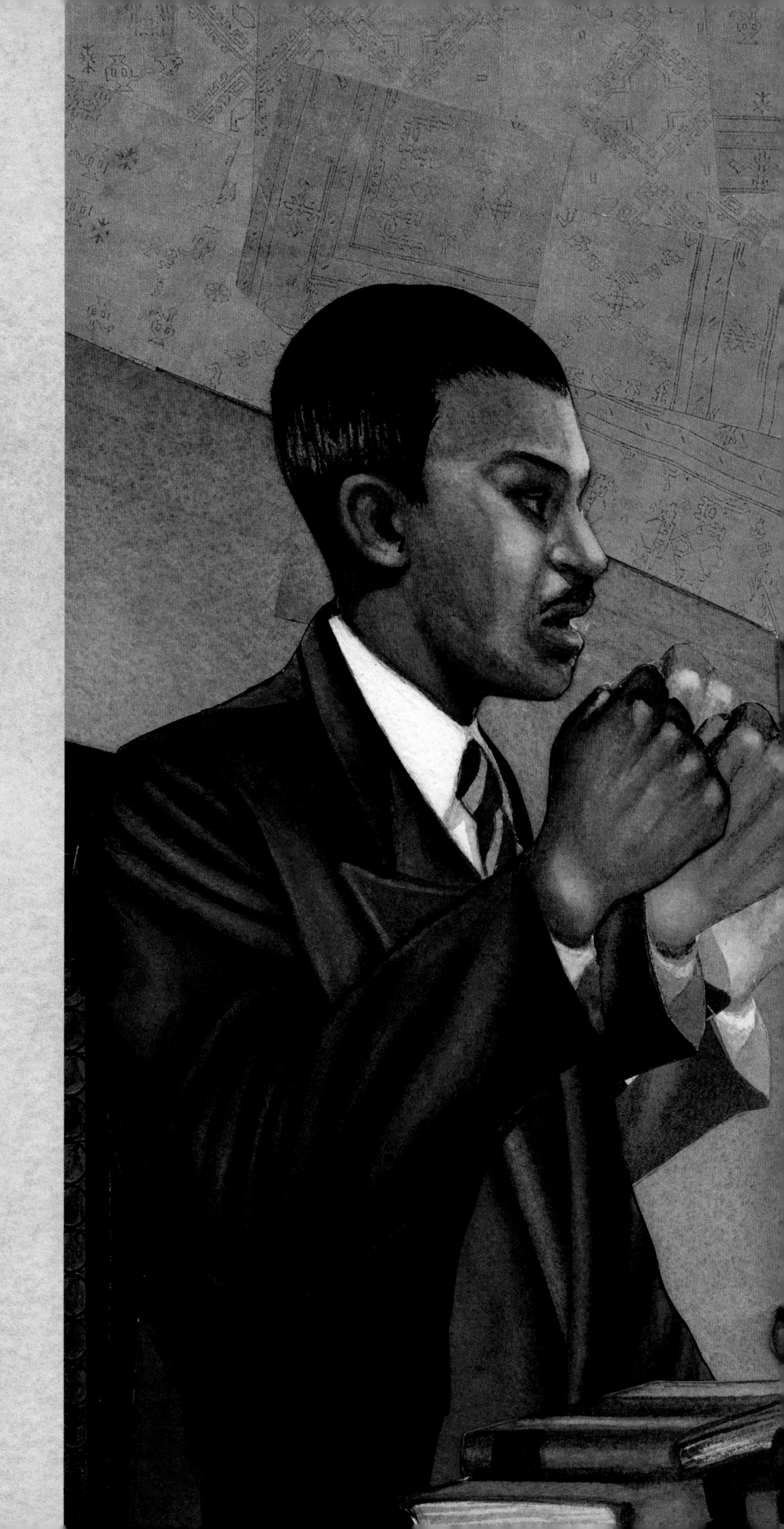

Because this was just a Maryland court case, its ruling didn't apply to the whole country. Still, it sure did impress the National Association for the Advancement of Colored People. In 1936, it hired him as a full-time lawyer at its headquarters in New York. Within two years, Thurgood was the NAACP's top lawyer.

FACT: In the South, Jim Crow laws required black people to drink from "colored" drinking fountains and sit in "colored" waiting rooms.

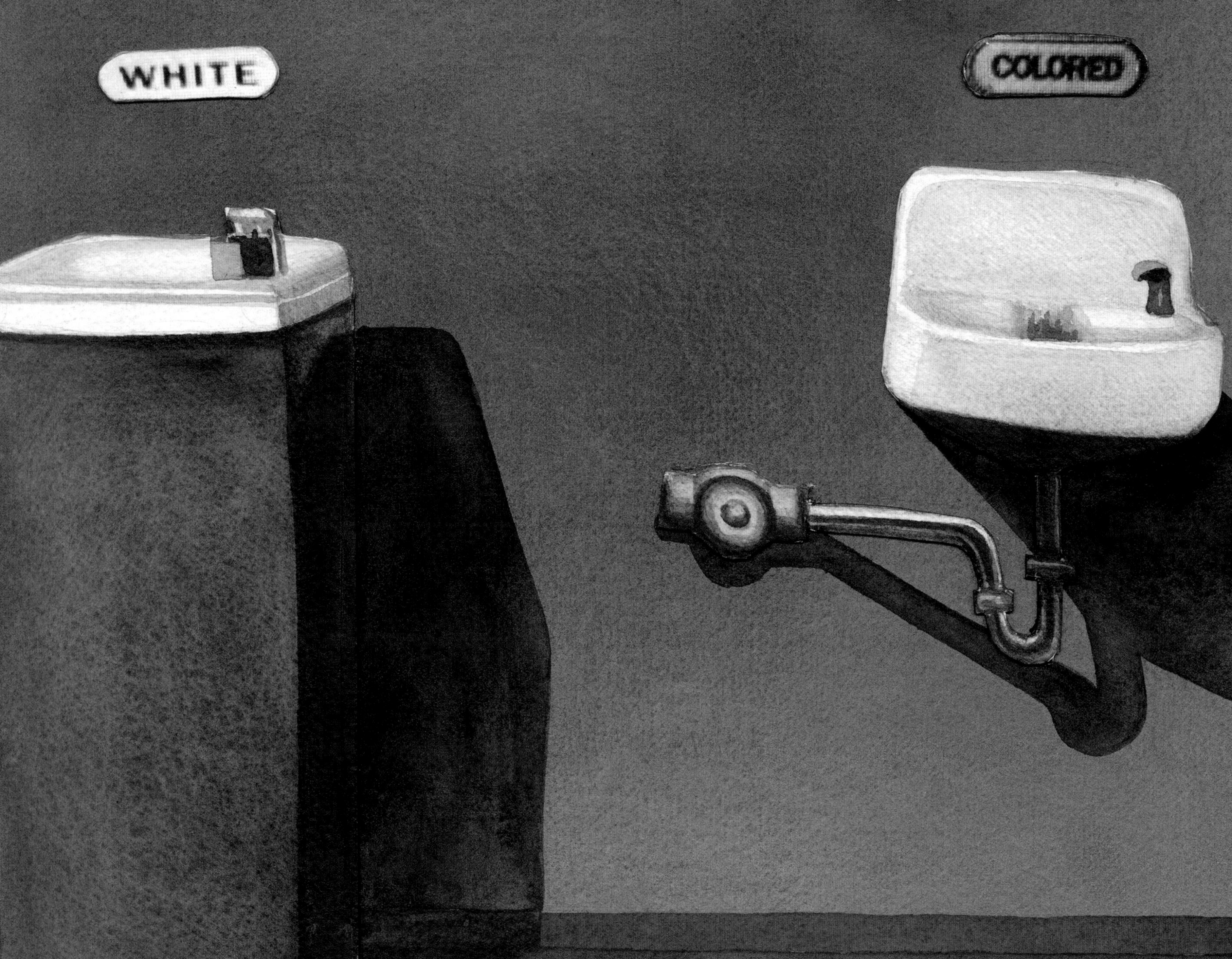

They were not allowed to vote. They were not allowed to eat in restaurants owned by whites, stay in hotels owned by whites, or sit where they wanted to on buses. This was the law. And Thurgood took it on.

FACT: On most trips Thurgood made to the South to fight a legal battle, there were threats to his life. Every night he had to eat and sleep in the house of a local black person. Sometimes there were armed guards posted outside. Was he scared? Darn right he was scared.

Once, in Tennessee, Thurgood was driving with some other lawyers down a country road when the police pulled them over. They arrested Thurgood, pushed him into their car, and took off.

The police car turned down a dirt road that led into the woods. When they got to a lake, Thurgood saw a group of white men just standing there, waiting. He knew they were planning to kill him.

Thankfully, the lawyers had followed. The police spotted them and turned around. Back at the station, they falsely charged Thurgood with drunk driving. He was released by the judge, then driven out of town by his friends in the dead of night.

THIS was the world Thurgood had to enter just to do his job.

FACT: In the Deep South, most whites sitting in courtrooms had never even seen a black lawyer. And there he was, in his fancy suit, trying to change their laws. It filled them with hatred. Thurgood's response was not anger—or none he let them see. No. Thurgood kept his cool. And in the midst of their hatred, Thurgood changed their laws, case by case, trial by trial, winning twenty-nine cases before the Supreme Court—cases that gained important rights for African Americans, cases that DEFINED the law of the land. Standing before those nine robed justices—nine white men—he took on INJUSTICE again and again. He fought for the equal protection of all citizens promised by the U.S. Constitution.

With every battle, Thurgood took a SLEDGEHAMMER to racial inequality in America. With every battle, he built his reputation as "MR. CIVIL RIGHTS," a nickname he earned by demolishing one racist law after the next. But his biggest battle was yet to come . . . and he had spent his whole life preparing for it.

INJUSTICE: A man named Oliver Brown attempts to enroll his children in an all-white school in Kansas—and they are rejected. If Thurgood can prove—in the Supreme Court—that the Brown children have a constitutional right to attend this school, he will have proven that all black children in America have the right to attend any public school.

When Thurgood stood up to present his argument, he spoke in a booming voice that filled the room. This case, this moment, was why he had been put on this earth—it was the most important battle he had ever fought. If he won, it would make all the difference—for millions of American schoolchildren, for the soul of the nation, for the ideal of racial justice in America. He came on like a locomotive.

Was he angry? After a lifetime of being treated like a second-class citizen because of the color of his skin? After enduring all that hatred, all those hurtful laws intended to keep black people powerless? DARN RIGHT HE WAS ANGRY.

But if he wanted to win this case, he had to prove his argument—word by word, point by point—with evidence.

Thurgood said that segregation "hurts the development of the personalities" of black children. It causes "humiliation" and "actual injury." He brought in psychologists to testify. He presented photographs of all-white schools and all-black schools. He argued that as long as there are separate schools, there can be no equality. He said, "Equal means getting the same thing, at the same time, and in the same place."

Listening to his powerful argument, seeing the injustice he described, every single one of those nine white Supreme Court justices agreed. Thurgood had won. The case of *Brown v. Board of Education* was decided. The age of legally separating black and white children in schools was over.

EQUAL JUSTICE

But Thurgood's career was far from over. He would go on to integrate more than just schools—by becoming the first black Supreme Court justice in history: **JUSTICE**.

AUTHOR'S NOTE

Thurgood Marshall was born on July 2, 1908, in Baltimore, Maryland, and died in Bethesda on January 24, 1993. The grandson of a slave, Marshall devoted his life to correcting America's long-standing racial injustice through the legal system. A forty-page picture book such as this cannot possibly convey the magnitude of his legacy. Not covered in this story are the criminal cases he argued, defending black clients who were victims of a racist criminal justice system in which they had to face police brutality, all-white juries, and unconstitutional state and local laws. Also not mentioned is Marshall's attempt to address lynching, the gruesome murder of black individuals by white gangs, usually by hanging. Lynching is a form of terrorism by which more than four thousand African Americans have been murdered. Marshall tried many times to get anti-lynching bills passed in the Senate. Despite his efforts, Southern senators managed to block them all.

The story of Marshall's ascent to the Supreme Court could be a book unto itself. As one of America's most respected lawyers, he was nominated to the U.S. Court of Appeals in 1961 by President John F. Kennedy—and confirmed by the Senate after months of resistance from Southern senators. In 1965, he was appointed by President Lyndon B. Johnson as America's Solicitor General—the highest government position that had ever been held by an African American. And on June 13, 1967, Johnson nominated Marshall to the Supreme Court—a nomination that faced major resistance from Southern senators. Despite their efforts, on August 30, Marshall was confirmed—and on October 2, he joined the Supreme Court as a justice, a position he held through his retirement on October 1, 1991.

As a member of the Supreme Court, Thurgood Marshall was the most outspoken advocate for racial justice in its history. He was also the Court's most outspoken critic of the death penalty, and wrote more than 150 dissenting anti-death-penalty opinions. As the years went by, Marshall more and more often found himself in the minority on the increasingly conservative court, earning himself the title "the Great Dissenter."

There is no single person in American history who contributed more to the cause of civil rights than Thurgood Marshall in terms of the sheer number of legal rights he secured through court battles. Starting in 1936 with the University of Maryland case (*Murray v. Pearson*) and continuing through the twenty-nine Supreme Court cases he won as the NAACP's top lawyer until 1961, his fourteen Supreme Court victories as Solicitor General, and his profound legacy as a Supreme Court justice, Marshall helped to make America "a more perfect union," to quote the U.S. Constitution. He was a giant.

Thurgood Marshall during *Brown v. Board of Education of Topeka*
Library of Congress Prints and Photographs, Visual Materials from NAACP Records, 1954.

Thurgood Marshall on the U.S. Supreme Court
by Robert S. Oaks for Library of Congress Prints and Photographs, 1976.